The Black Tide

by Nicole Parizeau

SEEDS OF SCIENCE

ROOTS OF READING™

Published and Distributed by

Delta Education
...because children learn by doing.®

A member of
School Specialty
Science

Published and Distributed by

A member of
School Specialty
Science

These materials are based upon work partially supported by the National Science Foundation under grant number ESI-0242733. The Federal Government has certain rights in this material. Any opinions, findings, and conclusions or recommendations expressed in this material are those of the author(s) and do not necessarily reflect the views of the National Science Foundation.

Developed at Lawrence Hall of Science and the Graduate School of Education at the University of California at Berkeley

Seeds of Science/Roots of Reading™ is a collaboration of a science team led by Jacqueline Barber and a literacy team led by P. David Pearson and Gina Cervetti.

Delta Education LLC
PO Box 3000
Nashua, NH 03061
1-800-258-1302
www.deltaeducation.com

The Black Tide
594-0007
ISBN-10: 1-59821-481-0
ISBN-13: 978-1-59821-481-9
1 2 3 4 5 6 7 8 9 10   11 10 09 08 07

Contents

Introduction

People use *a lot* of **oil**. We use oil to heat and light our homes. We use oil to make plastic. Gas is made from oil, and we use gas to run our cars.

We use oil in many ways.

Huge ships carry oil across the **ocean** to places where the oil is needed. These ships are so long that people can ride bicycles on them. The oil from just one ship could fill 900 classrooms!

Ships that carry oil can have accidents called oil spills. Sometimes an oil ship crashes on rocks near the **coast**. Or a storm breaks up the ship. These accidents cause oil to spill into the ocean. Large oil spills are terrible **disasters**.

This ship is carrying oil.

This book is about a real oil spill disaster that happened near the **shoreline** of Spain. Newspapers reported on the oil spill. Think about what will happen next as you read each newspaper story.

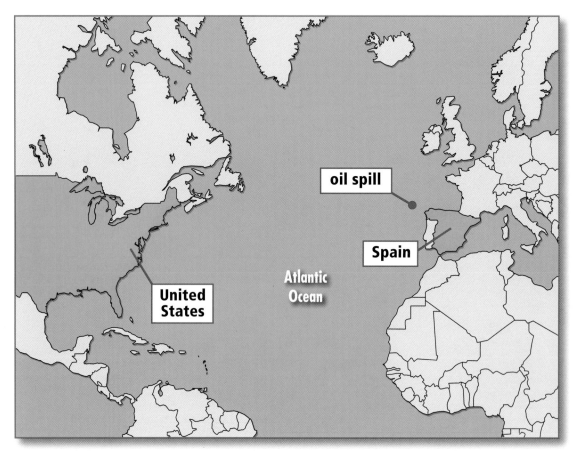

Oil spilled near Spain.

What Happened in the Ocean?

WORLD NEWS

November 13, 2002

SHIP FIGHTS STORM

This ship may sink.

SPAIN—An oil ship is in danger near the coast of Spain. A huge storm made a hole in the side of the ship. Wind and waves are rocking the ship. Some oil is spilling into the ocean.

OIL SHIP SINKS

The ship broke up after the storm.

SPAIN—The oil ship off the coast of Spain broke in half. The people from the ship are safe, but more thick oil is spilling into the ocean. The air smells like old eggs. Many dead fish are floating on the water. The ship is sinking.

OIL IN THE OCEAN

Oil spills can cover huge areas.

SPAIN—The oil spill is **harming** many **organisms** in the ocean. The oil will harm many more if it reaches the **shore**. Wind, waves, and **currents** are carrying oil toward the shore. Many **habitats** are in danger. Can people stop the oil before it reaches the shoreline?

OIL CLEANUP AT SEA

A barrier around the oil helps keep it from spreading.

SPAIN—Workers are trying to keep oil from the spill away from the shore. The workers put a huge floating **barrier** around the oil. The barrier is helping to keep the oil from moving around.

Workers collect oil from the water.

Now the workers are trying to **collect** the oil off the surface of the water. They scoop up oil. They also use nylon nets to collect the oil. The nets trap oil but let water through.

What Happened on the Shore?

WORLD NEWS

November 26, 2002

SHORELINE DISASTER

Waves carry oil onto the beach.

SPAIN—People could not stop the oil before it reached the shore. The **beaches** of Spain are black with oil. There is oil in the **seaweed** and oil in the **sand**. Rocks are black and oily.

Animals are covered with oil. Waves are carrying even more oil to the beach.

People are starting to clean up the shore. Cleanup will be a big job.

Spain needs help cleaning its beaches. This is a poster asking people to help.

December 3, 2002

OIL CLEANUP ON SHORE

People have to wash oil off one rock at a time.

People use pumps to suck oil off the beach.

SPAIN—It has been a week since the oil reached the shore. Many people are working to clean the sand and the rocks.

Cleaning up oil is a terrible job. Oil is hard to wash off anything it touches.

Sometimes the shore looks clean. Then the **tide** brings more oil to the beach. People call it a black tide.

ANIMALS IN DANGER

Oil hurts all shoreline animals that it touches.

SPAIN—**Scientists** are worried about the animals near the oil spill. Thousands of animals are covered with oil. Many animals are caught in the oil. They cannot move to find food.

Many **marine** animals have already died. Millions more are in danger.

Birds cannot fly if they are covered in oil.

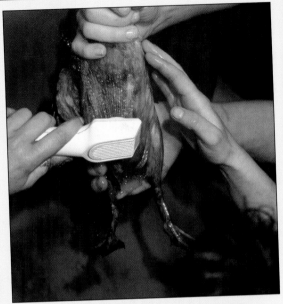

People use special soap to clean oil off animals. Oil is very hard to wash off.

Oil spills harm marine animals in many ways. Oil makes fur and feathers stick together. Birds can't fly with sticky feathers. **Sea otters** can't keep warm with sticky fur.

Some animals eat the oil when they try to clean themselves. Some eat food covered in oil. The oil makes them sick. Some cannot breathe through the oil.

Animals need to breathe, eat, and stay warm. If people can't clean the oil off the animals here, they will die.

WORLD 🌐 NEWS

January 19, 2003

OIL UNDER THE SAND

There is still oil under the sand.

SPAIN—The oil spill happened two months ago. The ocean looks clean now. But it still smells like old eggs. In some places, the sand looks clean. But if we dig under the surface, the sand looks oily and black. The oil is still there. Animals that make **burrows** in the sand cannot live here.

WORLD NEWS

November 19, 2003

IS OIL STILL HARMING THE SHORE?

Before the spill, Spain's beaches were clean and healthy.

SPAIN—One year ago, a ship spilled oil into the ocean near Spain. Is the shoreline clean yet? A team of scientists decided to find out. They **investigated** one part of the shoreline. They **compared** Spain's shoreline before and after the spill.

Millions of organisms died in the oil spill.

The scientists compared the number of organisms before and after the spill. They found **evidence** that more than 250,000 birds were killed in the oil spill. Many other kinds of organisms also died. The scientists found out that millions of organisms died in all.

Today the beaches in Spain look clean again. But there is still oil under the sand.

The scientists compared the sand before and after the spill. They said that people did a good job of cleaning oil from the surface of the sand. But the scientists found evidence of oil under the sand and rocks. The scientists said that oil under the sand can stay there for a long time. Sometimes storms or digging animals bring the oil to the surface.

Stopping oil spills from happening is even better than cleaning them up.

The scientists wrote a report to tell people what they learned. They hope their **investigation** will help people understand oil spills better. They want people to know that oil spills are hard to clean up. The scientists say that to keep shorelines clean, we need to stop spills from happening.

Can We Stop Oil Spills?

What happened near Spain could happen anywhere in the ocean. Oil spills happen all over the world. People use *a lot* of oil.

We can use less oil. We can drive less. We can turn off lights. We can use less plastic, which is made from oil. If *we* use less oil, *ships* will not carry so much oil. That means less oil will spill into the ocean . . . where it never really goes away.

We can do lots of little things to use less oil.